ESCAPE TO
Ireland

Photography by Simon Russell
Text by Anto Howard

Fodor's

FODOR'S TRAVEL PUBLICATIONS
NEW YORK • TORONTO • LONDON • SYDNEY • AUCKLAND • WWW.FODORS.COM

First Edition
ISBN 0-679-00788-1
ISSN 1533-5283

Special Sales

PRINTED IN GERMANY
10 9 8 7 6 5 4 3 2 1

Library of Congress Cataloging-in-Publication Data available
upon request.

Acknowledgments

From Simon Russell: Cheers to Anto, the best copilot in Ireland,
and to all his friends who appear in this book. Many thanks to
Rosemary Curran at Aer Lingus, and to Orla Carey and Maybeth
Fenton at the Irish Tourist Board, for all their help. For Jessica
Roth, who introduced me to Ireland, the biggest hug and kiss.
Thanks, Maebh and Tony, for the thrilling boat rides to the Aran
Islands and for my first swim with a dolphin. Pamela, for
introducing me to Fodor's. Hats off to Fabrizio and the Escape
team. And to Prabha and Alex, thanks for keeping an eye on my
little monster, Aidan, who waited patiently for Daddy's whiskery
kisses. And finally to my wife, Ann, thanks for letting me explore
the Emerald Isle and for keeping the home fires burning.

From Anto Howard: Thanks to the Ferriters, Paul, Brendan,
and pub-crawling Maurice; to Mark, Tom, Emma, Sid, Feargal, and
Clare; to Noel and Deirdre Comer for their hospitality and humor;
and to Tony and Maebh for making sense of County Clare. Thanks
to the O'Neills of Carnlough for the world's best pint; to Bert,
Robbie, Harry, John, Ray, and all the boys knee deep in the Bann;
to Olivia and family (especially Granny) and to Eileen in
Greenhaven. Thanks to Johnny and Mims for laughing through
the pain, to the Irish Landmark Trust and to Jim and Kate
Nicholson for their laid-back kindness, and to Jessie for her soup.
Thanks to Sinead and Aoibhe, the best discoveries of my summer.
Most of all, thanks to Simon for being a class act.

Credits

Creative Director and Series Editor: Fabrizio La Rocca
Editorial Director: Karen Cure
Art Director: Tigist Getachew

Editors: Christine Cipriani, Candy Gianetti
Editorial Assistant: Dennis Sarlo
Production/Manufacturing: C.R. Bloodgood, Robert B. Shields
Maps: David Lindroth, Inc.

Most books on the travel shelves are either long on the nitty-gritty and short on evocative photographs, or the other way around. We at Fodor's think the balance in this slim volume is just perfect, rather like the intersection of the most luscious magazine article and a sensible, down-to-earth guidebook. On the road, the useful pages at the end of the book are practically all you need. For the planning, roam through the color photographs up front: Each reveals a key facet of the corner of Ireland it portrays, and taken together with the lyrical accompanying text, all convey a sense of place that will take you there before you go. Each page opens up one of Ireland's most exceptional experiences; each spread leads you to the quintessential places that highlight the spirit of the Emerald Isle at its purest.

Some of these are sure to beckon. What's your pleasure? You may yearn to curl up in a tiny guest house—or lighthouse—and take tea as the mist gathers outside your lace-curtained window. You may dream of long, rowdy evenings at the pub, celebrating life, liberty, and the pursuit of Guinness. You may picture the rise and fall of a road winding gently over cliffs past heather, grass, and sea. Marvel at the barren, rocky Burren. Discover the landscape that inspired Donegal tweed. Dust off your Yeats and make for Ben Bulben. Taste fresh farmhouse cheese in West Cork. Drink in the unbearable greenness of it all.

To capture the magic of Ireland, we were inspired to throw local boy Anto Howard together with American photographer Simon Russell and let the island be their playground. They visited nearly every one of her 32 achingly beautiful counties, and slowly grew enchanted by this ancient place. By the time they had mountain-biked through the Connemara mountains, rolled down the lazy River Shannon on a barge, and meandered through Dublin's little streets in search of the perfect pint, it was impossible to tell native from visitor.

It has happened to centuries of travelers before them, and it will happen to you. So forget your projects and deadlines, and escape to Ireland. You owe it to yourself.

—The Editors

"YOU'RE A GENTLEMAN, A SCHOLAR. I'LL GO TO TWO THOUSAND."

"Oh, that's very generous, very kind. What about two and a half?"

"I can't argue with that, I can't. I'll give you two and a quarter?"

Since the early 16th century, farmers from the four corners of Ireland and beyond have gathered in this great open field to buy, sell, drink, dance, and, most of all, haggle. Protected in sturdy Wellingtons from dust, mud, and earthy remembrances from the more than 1,000 horses that roam the field—a moving fresco of browns, grays, and dappled white—you stand amid the throng of 10,000 traders with commerce on their minds. A strange harmony of human chatter and equine cries fills your ears, and the scent of leather and fresh sweat rides on the crisp October air. Sixteen-hand draft horses graze next to two-foot-tall Shetlands while handsome, rough

The Farmers' Holiday

THE BALLINASLOE HORSE FAIR AND SHOW

There's nothing a canny Irish horsetrader enjoys more than a long, hard haggle in the autumn rain.

Connemara ponies gallop alongside young Thoroughbred hunters. "Watch out there, sir!" A small, fearless child trots past, showing off his dad's prize cob before a likely buyer. Every last beast is for sale, and each has a little huddle around it—men shouting, laughing, spitting on their hands before slapping them firmly against another's in the shake that seals the deal. The faces are ruddy, wrinkled, sun-worn, the faces of men (and a few women) of the land. On the manicured lawn of the Show Ring, saddles are soaped and polished, metal bits glint, and you can see your face in the riders' leather boots. Berry-red and sea-green velvet jumpers' jackets flash about the arena, hurtling over hedge fences at deadly speed. Ladies in Victorian riding skirts canter sidesaddle. As the upper crust of the Irish horse world strut their stuff in the ring, next to you it's flat tweed caps and sweet-smelling pipes.

Sixteen-hand Irish drafts, tiny Shetlands, sturdy Connemara ponies, dappled cobs, wild Silkies—the fair is an equine Noah's ark of breeds and sizes, and the locals turn out in Sunday best to celebrate the wonder of it all.

On the velvety lawn
of the Show Ring it's all
about pride. You'll see
it in a spit-polished bit,
a brushed-velvet coat, the
neat binding of a tail,
and most of all in the
age-old pairing of rider
and steed as they vie to
be named best of breed.

STANDING ATOP THE 107 STEPS LEADING DOWN TO THE MAJESTIC Italianate gardens, you can picture it all: The year is 1796, and on the horizon beyond Bantry Bay, you, the future Earl of Bantry, have just spotted the tall white sails of the French fleet bringing invasion troops led by that Irish rebel Wolfe Tone. The warning must be given: "The French are coming! The French are coming!" You race across manicured lawn-tennis courts guarded by mythological statuary, past four stout cannons pointing out to sea, useless against such a force. Through the old rooms of the elegant manor house now, dashing past the stolen booty of generations of Anglo-Irish nobility. The figures seem to grin triumphantly down at you from Aubusson tapestries made for Marie Antoinette. "My sword, my steed!" you shout, then, like the devil, you ride the length and breadth

Earl for a Day

BANTRY HOUSE AND THE BEARA PENINSULA

The first Earl of Bantry built his great house and elegant grounds to proclaim to the world the power and sophistication of his family.

of your domain: the wild, sea-washed Beara Peninsula. Spreading the alarm, you pass through the Caha Mountains, ominous, tortured, all shifting patterns of light and shadow. Up narrow, treacherous Healy Pass, where rebel-friendly peasants peer out from tiny whitewashed cottages. Down steeply to the sea and the glimmering inlets dotted with isles of brush and rock. Through the fishing village of Castletownbere, where little boats lie docked side by side. But all the Southwest—the neighboring peninsulas of Iveragh and Dingle, equally tempting in their beauty and equally vulnerable to attack—must be warned. It is your duty. At last it's time to get back, for your treasure-packed house, wrapped in windows filled with candlelight, glows like a beacon to the wild Atlantic, a beacon calling the enemy to shore. Suddenly your vision clears—tonight, you recall comfortingly, you'll sleep in luxury within these walls, undisturbed by invaders from the sea.

The peasant claimed the untamed Beara Peninsula for his own. The heather was his crop, the beach his playground, the valleys his byways, and the ocean his dreams. Here he built a little whitewashed cottage, as dear to him as any lord's manor house.

An Island That Time Forgot

INIS MÓR, ARAN ISLANDS

THE FERRY LEAVES THE VIBRANT CITY OF GALWAY IN ITS WAKE, CROSSES 30 MILES OF BAY, AND LANDS you at the edge of the Atlantic on Inis Mór, a rough rock in a wild sea. The largest of the Aran Islands, it is a stark, flat landscape strewn with traces of Ireland before the heroes, the poets, the priests. Climb into one of the brightly painted pony carts waiting to meet the boats, and make your way to Dún Aengus, an Iron Age fort perched atop sheer 300-foot cliffs that fall away into the belligerent swells. From the center of its three perfectly concentric circles of gray-blue limestone the view is breathtaking: to the northeast, the Twelve Bens, rugged mountains of Connemara; to the south, Clare's moonlike Burren and the Cliffs of Moher, a 5-mile curtain of rock. In this most elemental of settings, you wonder who built this great fortress, and how. But it's one of the island's many mysteries. Like the head-high walls, some as old as Christ, that carve the treeless land into a jagged patchwork of brown and green laced with sinewy threads

Silence is the lord of Inis Mór, broken only by the rustle of the long grass, the roll of the sea, the soft laugh of an islander.

of stone. Unfathomable too that this remote, wind-whipped place was a cradle of early Irish civilization. At Na Seacht d'Teampaill, seven churches (now ruins) and high Celtic crosses hacked out of stone signaled the end of the ancient ways. In the fishing village of Kilronan, the faces around you smile, but there's a hardness in the eyes, a fierce independence. Hard-living people, families here for scores of generations, they speak in Irish with an accent and idioms not taught in any school. Near the beach at Kilmurvey, where gray seals dive and flip in the shallows, there's an old farmhouse—stone, of course—where a peat fire's blazing and a hot meal awaits you on the great oak table: lamb reared on these bare hills, potatoes grown in this rocky ground. More mysteries still.

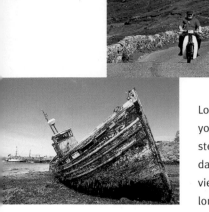

THE WARNING PASSES QUICKLY DOWN THE CHAIN AS YOU ALL meander out of the hamlet of Finny after a light tea at the Happy Kettle: "Pothole! Pothole!" This is easy, you tell yourself, grinning, as you coast on your ultramodern mountain bike around serene Lough Nafooey's coastal backroads. Then the land starts to rise, and rise again. Before you know it, you and your new friends are locked in a first-gear battle at the foot of the stern Maumturk Mountains. Out of breath, teeth clenched, you rain curses on this damned, ancient hill. But, oh, once you crest it, the reward is great indeed: a stunning view of Killary Harbour, Ireland's only fjord, splitting the silent mountains and the lonely old town of Leenane nestled beneath them. Now the wild descent, the yelps of your fellow speedsters, and you fly past a bus party. Fools, encased in their cage of

The Agony and the Ecstasy

BIKING THROUGH THE HILLS OF CONNEMARA

To cycle in the Maumturk Mountains is to be alone in an elemental place, with prehistoric rocks and pleasant thoughts for company.

metal and glass! On your bike you can smell the lemony Sitka spruce, hear the curlew's plaintive cry, see the sun play on the sky-bright waters, taste the thick, sea-salted air that locals say builds a mighty appetite. There's proof in the evening, at the stately Georgian Rosleague Manor, where the day's endeavor is dissected around a dinner table fat with fish, lamb, and fowl. Amid the smell of the peat fire and the whisper of waves at nearby Ballinakill Bay, mock fear mixes with fake bravado in tales of conquering the cruel highlands of the least inhabited region in Ireland. In this land of myth, heroic bruises are brandished with pride over port and brandy. Has everyone forgotten that you ride again tomorrow?

A bike goes everywhere...
Locals look on in head-
scratching wonder as those
"two-wheeled madmen" roll
slowly into every nook and
cranny of wild Connemara.
The hills can't stop them,
nor the water, nor the sand,
but the pubs in the character-
strewn village of Leenane
may hold them for a while.

LOST IN A SOFT SWELL OF HANDSEWN LINEN AND FINE COTTON QUILTS, you awaken. Your eyes clear, then focus on the ceiling so high above. The glittering chandelier! The gilded plasterwork! Where are you? The light is a clue, flooding in as it does through the great half-moon windows, setting aglow the white and yellow paneled walls and the polished wood of an antique French wardrobe. The room looks like the inside of a wedding cake. The window draws you toward it, and, still blinking, you look out onto Fitzwilliam Terrace and Square. It's early morning, and traffic is light...for a moment you could be back in the "gorgeous eighteenth," those magical hundred years after 1720 that saw Dublin transformed from ugly duckling to the envy of Europe. It's all there before you, little changed—the commodious, uniform

A Window onto an Elegant Past

A GUEST HOUSE IN GEORGIAN DUBLIN

The city's Georgian town houses were built to welcome the sun through huge floor-to-ceiling windows and the colorful front doors' fanlights.

streets; the genteel town squares centered on lush little parks; the redbrick mansions, their doors brightly lacquered in black, red, yellow, green. The sun catches each and glints off the open-mouthed-gargoyle brass knockers and the Adamesque fanlights above. A knock on the door and you're stirred from your daydream. "Breakfast on the terrace," announces the cheery voice of Noel, your host. There's no doubt now: You're in the yellow room at Number 31, a most refined guest house in a tiny mews at the heart of Georgian Dublin. Later—as you prepare to leave your elegant nest and emerge into a "tapestry of rosy brick and white enamel," as Horace Walpole called the area between Fitzwilliam and Merrion squares—the spirit of an age past seems to whisper a happy command: "You will stroll without hurry through these peaceful streets, and stop only for the taking of tea."

Genteel St. Stephen's Green was the center of a favorite 18th-century Beaux Walk, where the families of the upper classes strolled in all their finery.

SET YOUR WATCH TO SHANNON TIME (THAT'S REAL SLOW) AS the *Shannon Princess* casts off from the 13-arched stone bridge at Killaloe for a trip up the old spine of Ireland. Captain Ruairí Gibbons, gruff but warm, stands tall in the wheelhouse as the Dutch barge meanders through the fjordlike reaches of the lower Shannon and into lovely Lough Derg. With a bow, Ruairí hands you the wheel. Steady as she goes. The boat rocks softly as it passes the round tower on Holy Island, easing your mind into the meditative state of Saint Cáinín and his 7th-century monks, who renounced the world to live there. Bankside fishermen smile at you, the calm of the river in their eyes. Your six-day voyage, from Clare in the west up to Athlone at the very center of the country, passes through many sacred lands of early Christian Ireland, a time

Queen of the River

A BARGE TRIP ON THE SHANNON

Silent and still, the eons-old river remains undisturbed as the pristine barge *Shannon Princess* glides gently through its indigo waters.

when mystic and chieftain lived side by side, drawn to the water of life. Olivia, wife to the skipper and a Cordon Bleu–trained chef, calls you down for lunch, served family-style with your fellow travelers. Throughout the sumptuous meal your eyes are drawn out the window to the wooded shore. There the earthen mounds of Beal Ború and Griananlaghna, the Bronze Age settlement of Crannog, creep silently by, ghosts of long-dead generations half-hidden in the trees. On deck in the evening, you watch the barge pass through Portumna Swing Bridge before the obliging waters of Meelick Lock lift it onto the next stretch of Ireland's greatest river. At the end of the long, gentle day, after pondering the constellations hung in the crystal-clear sky, you retire to your snug cabin, lulled to sleep by the rhythmic lapping against the bow outside your window. Mother Shannon takes care of her children.

While skipper Ruairí Gibbons steers the old Dutch barge through rushing lock and placid lake, the passengers gather below with local musicians for an evening of *craic*—that's Irish for drink, song, and laughter. Outside the portholes, the blue of water and sky, constant companions, slowly fades to black.

snug about waking up sheltered within meter-thick granite walls. Standing in the center of your octagonal bedroom, you turn slowly, surveying the bright greens, the dark blues, the virgin whites of land, sea, and sky that fill each large porthole window. By its very nature, the lighthouse out on Wicklow Head has a spectacular view over both coastline and sea. To the west, you look out on Avondale Forest Park and the sheep-dotted, wild-grass hills around Rathnew. To the south, a pair of lovers meanders along a silver strand of beach toward rocky Ardmore Point. To the north, across Brittas Bay, lies bustling Wicklow Town. And to the east, watched over by the new automated lighthouse, is the lapis lazuli expanse of the Irish Sea. A hundred feet

Closer to Heaven

A LIGHTHOUSE STAY ON WICKLOW HEAD

The towering Wicklow Lighthouse is the perfect place to hide away from the world, alone with your thoughts or with a companion at your side.

above mere mortals, in a bliss of solitude and pin-drop quiet, you think back on the sea-hardened men who once worked in this tower, close to the gods in their omnipercipience, guarding unknown mortals from venturing too near these shores. After a warm, scent-filled morning bath in the iron tub, you climb the spiral staircase to join your housemates for breakfast in the intimate, oven-heated kitchen. Stepping outside your isolated stone sentry, you revel in the elemental freedom of uncluttered space, then set off for a constitutional on the now-deserted beach, perhaps a drive into the wooded Wicklow Mountains with a stop at the azalea-strewn Mount Usher Gardens. After dinner in some little bistro on one of the town's narrow streets, you're back in the kitchen, praying for the one thing that would make your stay here among the clouds complete: a wild, sky-rending, wave-rearing, froth-whipping storm. "Blow winds, crack your cheeks!"

YOU'VE PLAYED COURSES FROM PEBBLE BEACH TO ST. ANDREWS, BUT you've seen nothing quite like the contorted patchwork of grass, sand, and water you view from the balcony of the Royal Portrush clubhouse. Shaped by the sea to torment the amateur, bring down the braggadocio, and reward the patient, the neighboring links of Royal Portrush and Portstewart should list Mother Nature as course designer. A glutton for punishment could play both in one day—they're barely a wayward five-iron apart down a sunny coast road. On the first tee at Portrush, you watch seagulls flying low over the dunes, the reeds motionless in the water. The sun is warm on the scorched grass, and the ruins of Dunluce Castle look sleepily down from their hill. Safe enough, you decide, and swing aggressively. Aha! The wind was waiting for you! The rolling terrain makes every lie

Tee and Sympathy

MASTERING THE LINKS OF NORTHERN IRELAND

Leave pride at home—
at Portrush the wind
is deceitful, the rough is
tricky, and the game
comes second to the
stroll with Mother Nature.

seem downhill, and the thick grass is merciless, gobbling up balls like a carpet of Venus flytraps. The greens, fast as lightning, shake off your perfect approach as a dog would a flea. Now you're in the bunker, the sand soft and sucking, the lip high and mocking. For a moment you contemplate the awesome shot to come. A fellow sufferer on the next fairway throws you a sympathetic smile, as kind as the course is spiteful. The low sun makes a silhouette of the hills as they flow down to the royal blue sea. The strong smell of the brine prompts the first stirring of an appetite. You recall what you heard about the "great Ulster fry"—a sausage-and-bacon-laden pub lunch—and the fellow in the clubhouse who said, "The pint's not bad 'round these parts." A stroll on the Victorian boardwalk after the game would be nice.... The shot? You fluffed it, but never mind. All's well with the world.

"LISTEN TO HIM PLAY THAT FIDDLE, THAT TOMMY PEOPLES. Look at the face on him, wild, ungodly, lost in damned music. Some say he sold his soul to the Devil to play that well." It's the Fleadh Nua—Ennis's annual five-day binge of traditional Irish music—and all afternoon the streets, pubs, and halls have crackled with rumors of the great ones turning up tonight. Peoples, they all whispered, was the man to see. Head to Cruise's bar around eight. So here you are, watching as one amazing player after another appears out of the cigarette mist and takes a seat in the great pagan circle. Tommy's big leather boot taps out four to start things off with a lively reel. The whine of the strings enters first—the fiddles, a mandolin, a banjo—and then, one by one, the ethereal wooden flute, the piercing tin whistles, the droning uilleann pipes and wheezy

The Music of Ancients

FLEADH NUA, IRISH MUSIC FESTIVAL AT ENNIS, COUNTY CLARE

For one heady week in May, everything in Ennis has a rhythm: Every foot taps, every girl dances, and everybody takes a turn at making music.

button accordion. From a whisper to a storm, the beat—underscored by the relentless rapping of the taut-stretched goatskin bodhran—and the sad, sweet melody pick up pace and volume until your very blood seems to pulse with a new rhythm. The walls can't hold it now; the music flows out the window and into the night. From every other bar and street in town more sounds emerge, as if every brick and cobble were bleeding music. Through the window you see street dancers line up to face each other, a glorious display. A kick of hornpipe shoes and they're off, a controlled ballet of young free spirits. Here inside, random couples form—child with old man, woman with woman, boy with girl—and there's no way you're sitting still. An old woman motions to you to join her. The word "no" means nothing; she pulls you to your feet and twirls you into the madness. Tommy Peoples grins.

The face of a skilled traditional musician
in full flight is a study in concentration and
bliss. All around, the old become young,
the seated rise to dance, and the single quickly
find a partner.

"OUT OF THE WAY, THERE, LANDLUBBER!" CRIES THE CAPTAIN AS a death-cold wash of Atlantic spray catches you in the face. What am I doing here? you ask yourself. It all made sense last night in the pub. Through the sailors' haze of pipe smoke, you saw the wide smile of Dr. Michael Brogan, skipper of a 40-foot hooker in tomorrow's big race, and mentioned your interest in the sea. The shake of a hand, a round of drinks, and the deal was done—he asked only that you revel in the thrill of it. Now 20 Galway hookers, their wooden bows low in the water, fill the wine-dark bay. A few pristine white sails, but mostly dark, mysterious calicos, rust brown, charcoal gray, pure black—a nod to the days when tree-bark dyes were used to stiffen the sheets. The colors of tradition, for that's what the Gathering of the Boats is all about: remembering a time when the

Gathering of the Boats

THE REGATTA AT KINVARA, COUNTY GALWAY

In this meeting of the Galway hookers—less of a race, more of a dance— rusty red calicos flirt with one another as sailors exchange friendly jibes.

boatmen of Connemara plied the bay in these triple-sailed fishing smacks, bringing turf from the bogs to trade for provisions and making friends along the way. From the jetty, the censer-wielding priest blesses boat and navigator alike: *"Dia dhibh, Dia dhibh."* God bless. The gun sounds and you're off, gliding at some speed as the crew, men and women of the West, tack sharply and boat vies with boat—at most a length apart—for the heart of the blow. Back toward town in the last, desperate leg of the race, you see Dunguaire Castle atop a rise, and beyond that the mournful hills of the Burren. Picnicking families cheer every boat as it coasts in. Is that music you hear? They're already warming up in Brogan's pub for the night ahead. "How did we do, Skipper?" you ask. But nobody seems to know...or care.

For some, the Gathering is about an unbroken tradition, the age-old link between man and sea and a century-old one between Galway and Connemara. For others, it's the thrill of a high-speed tack across an opponent's bow.

But for most, it's the beauty of red,
white, and lacquered brown sails
cutting across the endless blue of
Galway Bay.

WHAT STIRS? VOICES WAKE YOU IN THE NIGHT—MEN GROWLING, drinking, plotting war and bloody mayhem. The clank of chain mail, the whinny of nervous horses. Quickly you spring from your bed and step out the front door of your fisherman's cottage. Grass beneath your feet, soft, a touch of dew. Not a soul about. The full moon clears the clouds and lights up the tiny village of Slade. From gray to white to silver, it transforms the walls of the ruined castle that peers down scornfully at your cozy little dwelling. The voices? You were dreaming, of course, of Strongbow, greatest of the Norman invaders, and his lords. Earlier in the day you walked with the kids along Baginbun Bay, where those fearless conquerors of Celtic Ireland landed more than 800 years ago. What plans were hatched where you now stand? In this very yard, where sun-rosy Irish

In Strongbow's Shadow

A COTTAGE STAY IN THE SOUTHEAST

Towering over the little cottages, the stern, deserted castle reminds you that this was once Norman land, where the sword and the steed held sway.

children frolicked with your own, how many proud sons of Normandy stood learning to swing a long sword, to tame a horse? A smell jolts you from your dreams, salt in the night air, and a noise—the brackish water lapping against the bows of brightly colored trawlers not 50 yards from your door. Your mouth moistens, and your belly remembers its last meal: a thick fish soup made from the random wonders of the day's catch, soaked up with half a loaf of the local soda bread. A meal fit for a lord indeed. Back in the fire-warmed cottage, your family sleeps on, oblivious, and the stuffed owl grins down at you, mocking your wild imagination. Behind you, a new cloud blankets the moon, and the lowering, ancient castle returns to the darkness and to history.

Slade is the quintessential fishing village.
The pace is slow. Life revolves around the sea,
at once generous friend and unknown danger.
And, in the still of the night, young boys dream
of a life of adventure on an ocean wild and free.

Eating Your Greens

IN SEARCH OF THE FARMHOUSE CHEESE OF WEST CORK

GREEN, ALL ABOUT YOU IN GUBBEEN'S HIGH FIELD. NO, NOT GREEN—GREENS, A TAPESTRY OF SUBTLE shades, darker under the blackberry bushes; dappled where the sun breaks through the sycamore trees; lighter, almost emerald, in the pasture where you stand. Farther afield, atop Mount Gabriel to the north, the green is pale, almost yellow. Even the wild sea of Roaringwater Bay: blue? No, race-car green. It's the color of Ireland, of course, but so many tones! You bend your knee, run your fingers through the silky grass. This is how Ireland looks, feels, smells.... You catch the scent on the wind like the past, like a school morning. To taste it—that's what you desire. To taste the whole lush, wonderful country! You've come to the right place, the epicenter of a region devoted to the glories of farmhouse foods, where the relationship between the landscape and the fruits it yields is intimate, almost sensual. What's that you see in the corner of the field? A lone cow, short and jet

The long-horned Kerry cow is a magical machine for turning the emerald green grasses of Gubbeen Farm into a plate of pungent, deep yellow, hard-rind cheese.

black, long horns bowed as it mechanically chews its cud. An unimpressive breed, you sniff...but wait. Look closely. It's the answer to your wishes. From this wee Kerry cow—crossbred for decades by Tom Ferguson, fattened on the grass beneath your feet—flows some of the creamiest milk in the world. Add a little prime millet, years of local lore, and the mystic, loving touch of Tom's wife, Giana, and you have it: Gubbeen's hard-rind cheese. Hold it in your hand: solid as Cork limestone, cool as the River Lee. The scent rises to tempt you: wild mushrooms with some whisper of ancient oak. "A deep yellow," the brochure says, "almost orange," but you know better: It's green, a great ball of living Ireland.

TAKE NO MAP WITH YOU TO WILD, WIND-SHAPED SLIGO; THE collected works of Yeats will do. As boy and man, the great urbane artist came here to play, to breathe, to imagine a simpler life. The place ran through his soul like the blood through his veins, and every lake, wood, and hill left its tracks across his poetry. You can hear him on the wind, cantankerous as ever, telling you where to go, what to see. Start atop Ben Bulben, a stark, flat-topped mount visible from every point around: Here Diarmuid and Gráinne fled for sanctuary, mythical lovers as doomed as Yeats and the ice-cool Maud Gonne. Hike down there, he orders, where castle and church meet at the edge of gentle Lough Gill. Stand and look out at the misty, mystical "Lake Isle of Innisfree," where the poet dreamed of living alone "in the bee-loud glade." Listen to the "lake water lapping with

In the Poet's Footsteps

COUNTY SLIGO: YEATS COUNTRY

"Under bare Ben Bullben's head, in Drumcliff churchyard Yeats is laid..." Not London, nor Dublin, but simple Sligo Yeats chose as his eternal resting place.

low sounds by the shore" until, like him, you "hear it in the deep heart's core." Suddenly he's pulling you west through the raw, sensual landscape to Rosses Point and a vast sandy beach where children frolic as he once did. South, then, to Knocknarea—a hill older than God, they say. There, place your hand on the massive, stone-heaped cairn where "passionate Maeve," warrior queen of Connaught, is rumored to be buried. Can you feel her? In these rocks, these hills, lie the eons-old stories that sang to him, urging him to his pen. Coming full circle now, he leads you to the foot of Bulben, to Drumcliffe, where his great-grandfather was church rector. Here, in the oak-sheltered graveyard beside an ancient round tower, he departs with a few last words—his self-penned epitaph, chiseled onto the stone slab that marks his resting place: "Cast a cold eye on life, on death. Horseman, pass by!"

Yeats's poetry was inspired by the epic landscape of Sligo's forests, mountains, seashore; by the grandeur of houses like Lissadell ("Great windows open to the south,/ Two girls in silk kimonos, both/ Beautiful, one a gazelle"); and by Innisfree, the moody lake isle.

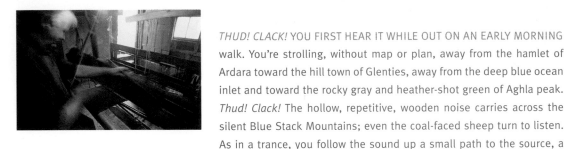

THUD! CLACK! YOU FIRST HEAR IT WHILE OUT ON AN EARLY MORNING walk. You're strolling, without map or plan, away from the hamlet of Ardara toward the hill town of Glenties, away from the deep blue ocean inlet and toward the rocky gray and heather-shot green of Aghla peak. *Thud! Clack!* The hollow, repetitive, wooden noise carries across the silent Blue Stack Mountains; even the coal-faced sheep turn to listen. As in a trance, you follow the sound up a small path to the source, a humble white and red shack roofed in tin. A sheepdog lies half asleep in the doorway, waiting patiently for whistle and call to begin the workday. *Thud! Clack!* The door is open, and you peep into the dimly lit room where Peter McGuire—a slight man, but all muscle—commands shuttle, warp, and weft on his huge old loom. For

Weaving the Elements

A COTTAGE STAY IN THE LAND OF DONEGAL TWEED

Weavers like Francis O'Donnell (above) work alone and in quiet, the only sounds the *clack* of the warp and the whistle of the wind across nearby Naran Strand.

50 years he has woven Donegal tweed, nothing else, an art as old as civilization, and now a dying one. In the great sheets of cloth rolling in slow-motion waves from this man and his machine, you see reflected all the colors of the rugged landscape: the green meadows of lush Dunmore Head, the browns and whites of the bogs and Naran Strand, the steely gray of the Slieve League Cliffs, the flecks of heather purple and berry red. Donegal tweed is a tapestry of this coastal haven, hard and durable, full of color and spirit. In days gone by, when there were 300 weavers hereabouts and not 20, they would boil turf, mud, grass, and nettles to dye the cloth, Peter tells you as he walks you back to his cottage for a cup of tea. Take no photos of Donegal, buy no books about the place; simply purchase a good tweed scarf—map and memento of this wild, rugged corner of the world.

Donegal tweed is spun from the
great wheel of the landscape
around the village of Ardara: the
hues of sea and mountain, of bog
and strand, the texture of wild
grass and rough heather. In a
skilled and patient weaver's
hands these elemental ingredients
are tamed and transformed.

THE ROCK AND THE HARD PLACE. THERE'S NO WAY AROUND THAT wall—you'll all have to go back. But Shane Conolly, humble farmer and guide, begins to remove a small section of that millennium-old pile of loose stones with his big, shovel-like hands. Everyone passes through the new gap, and Shane, with great care, replaces every rock just as he found it. Let there be no doubt: The man is at one with this strange, untamed land. Now on you walk behind him, into the fierce, lunar landscape of the Burren—An Bhoireann, the "rocky place"—as steely gray as the rest of Ireland is green. Before you, as far as the eye can see, is a mosaic of karst: vast, irregular slabs of limestone with earth-deep cracks between them. "Neither water enough to drown a man, nor tree to hang him, nor soil to bury him" is how one of Cromwell's officers described the Burren. Out here you

Walking on the Moon

THE BURREN, COUNTY CLARE

A vast ocean of gray rock, the Burren is a landscape more lunar than terrestrial, a silent world built for solitude.

can see for miles, all the way to the daunting Cliffs of Moher, and you seem to be the only living thing. But nature has somehow sculpted life into the inanimate rock. The carpet of dull green shale and bright gray limestone rises and falls, moving like dark waves on an ocean. The world about you is huge, somehow terrible, as if you are lost in a silent storm. Bringing you back to earth, Shane whispers in your ear, "The mark of man is here too." He points to the miles of stone walls, nods east toward the 7,000-year-old burial monuments of Poulnabrone Dolmen and the immovable wedge tomb of Gleninsheen. At least six megalithic tombs are erected in this barren place on the higher land where civilization began. For eons it has been sacred to all, understood by none. Shane Conolly gives it a good go all the same.

The Celtic Irish have always held sacred this limestone wasteland that runs from the mountains down to the crystal sea. Hard to imagine that 6,000 years ago it was covered in light forest, its rich soil lost to erosion when farmers cleared the trees and overgrazed the grasses, exposing the rock below.

Dublin's Black Blood

A PUB CRAWL ALONG THE RIVER LIFFEY

YOUR FIRST GULP (NEVER A SIP) IS A LITTLE BITTER GOING DOWN, BUT THE TEXTURE WINS YOU OVER to the dark side—cream on the lip, velvet on the tongue, chocolate in the throat. As you imbibe, the thick white head leaves rings of pleasure down the glass: footprints of quality. Reluctantly you put the pint down, but the moment is not quite over. A warm tickle on the upper lip calls out to your tongue, which darts out to remove, in one slow sweep, the temporary mustache of the world's best stout. If a city is a living thing, Dublin's heart is powered by the huge pumps of the Guinness factory at St. James's Gate, and its blood is black as night and thick as soup. The stuff of life flows east along the Liffey into the thousand pubs that bless and curse every street and lane. With a tribute to the source— a stop at Guinness's own pub and museum—you and your comrades begin the ritual. The Liffey ushers you through her city to her finest bars, famed for perfect pints of the black stuff. Decor ranges

How do you get from one side of Dublin to another without passing a pub? You go into every one!

from the spit and sawdust of Ryans to the Victorian marble of the Stag's Head; the clientele, from cloth-capped old-timers to fine young things. But one thing is constant: Nectar has nothing on the divine brew you're knocking back. Somewhere between two pubs on the Liffey quays, your tongue loosens, your arm tightens around a friend, and the river shimmers with the lights of the city. The names of the bars, full of romance in themselves and vaguely familiar from the novels of Joyce, slowly roll into one—the Brazen Head, the Temple Bar, Davey Byrnes, and on through the warm Dublin night. Around 11, last drinks are called. Funny how everyone always looks so handsome about now.

YOUR CAR CRESTS A STEEP HILL AT TORR HEAD, AND ALL YOU SEE is open sky. For a moment, you're ready to fly. Suddenly the descent, and before you loom the white sand shore of Murlough Bay and the turquoise North Channel beyond. A car rounds a corner coming from the opposite direction. By all the laws of nature, two cars cannot possibly pass on these slender roads snaking the Antrim Coast, yet pass you do, with a wave, each vying to give way to the other. Then on you go, rising and falling with the contours of the land, soothed by the rhythmic verse of nine little valleys passing in turn: Glenarm, Glen of the Weapon, Glencorp, Glen of the Slaughter.... The pleasure of driving the Glens is stopping, and the pleasure of stopping is knowing you'll soon move on. Into Glenariff, loveliest of the Glens, you plunge, wondering at the carpet-

Over Hill and Dale

A DRIVE ALONG THE ANTRIM COAST THROUGH THE GLENS

Always to your right as you meander along the coast, the dark blue sea of the cliff-rimmed North Channel calls the locals out to play.

smoothness of the hills, the feline grace of their curves. What a craftsman, that old glacier, you think. What a landscape artist. From Carnlough north to the Giant's Causeway—a spectacular mass of volcanic rock pillars spilling into the Atlantic, created as stepping stones by the giant Finn McCool to help him reach his beloved on the isle of Staffa—the sea always whispers from the right: the voice of the fisherman and smell of the brine calling you out for a swim, a stroll, a bath in the summer sun. From the left, forests of ash, beech, and oak are other sirens, suggesting picnic-perfect meadows, hikes between 22 waterfalls, climbs culminating in vistas over the rolling farmland and rivers of the North. Little fishing towns—Cushendun, Glenariff, Ballintoy—hold temptations, too: fairy-tale tea shops with warm scones light as a cloud and fruity jam sponges thick as doorsteps. Food, you decide, licking sticky lips, always tastes better by the sea.

Stop and paint them or just drive by in wonder, but the nine lovely Glens of Antrim, winding lazily between the Antrim Hills and out into the welcoming sea, refuse to be ignored. Evenings of cakes and ale await in the pristine seaside villages.

The history of Ulster is the
history of Ireland: from
the prehistoric magnificence
of the Giant's Causeway,
to the medieval might of
walled Dunluce Castle, to
the Carrick-a-Rede rope
bridge, which has granted
local fishermen passage
for generations.

Dance of the Fly

FLY FISHING THE RIVERS BANN AND AGIVEY

IT'S A TALE OF TWO RIVERS AND TWO MASTERS, BOTH GHILLIES—ALL-KNOWING GURUS OF THESE pristine northern waters, men whom fish fear. At dawn you're knee-deep in a pool at Carnroe with one of them, amid the rapid, hissing waters of the wide Lower Bann. On Robbie's whispered word you send your Gary-dog fly into the swirl below the wild weir where the great silver-bullet salmon, new to the river this season, rest before attempting their Great Leap Forward. Strutting its gaudy colors, the man-made insect dances to your tune across the sparkling surf. The fish aren't biting yet, but Robbie's wit is. An unlit Woodbine hanging from his mouth, he's sharp as a hook, fast and mercurial as the Bann, and with fish tales, local history, even a bit of gossip, he keeps you chuckling all the long day—mostly at yourself. Then, when you least expect it, the electric thrill of a tug on your line. "Someone's knocking," says Robbie

In the silver water of the Bann there rages a war between angler and salmon where the sword is a whipping rod and the bullet a wickedly colorful fly.

as the fight begins. Twilight finds you on a grassy bank of the narrow Agivey River, sheltered by a canopy of sycamores amid an ancient wood. A rabbit—not startled, simply out to stretch his legs—scurries past your feet. A man in a soft felt hat stands at your side, saying little but always smiling. He talks now and then of the fish: where they spawn, where they gather, what they like to eat. He jokes about their guile. Bert's humor is as slow and meandering as his unhurried Agivey. Fishing is not about the fish, he tells you, but all about the river, time spent by the water among things green and wild. His soothing voice is interrupted by the tilt of your rod as a fat old salmon calls for your attention.

ON YOUR FIRST MORNING IN HORSE COUNTRY, YOU'RE awakened by the shrill whinny of a stallion in the lush front field. From the sash window of the master bedroom in Lismacue House you look down on three generations of Nicholsons—latest in a line here since 1704—heading off to their stables. Saddle, bit, and bridle, all polished and crisp, are dutifully taken from their hooks; horse boxes are entered; and the group reappears, transformed, regal, a family born to the saddle. Walk turns to trot and, with a gentle kick, to canter as the beasts carry the Nicholsons down the endless avenue of limes. Everyone in south Tipperary seems to ride—look down at passing feet in Bansha and you're sure to spot a few pairs of riding boots. You too have caught the bug. In the afternoon you find yourself aboard Major, a surefooted

Life in the Saddle

RIDING IN THE GALTEE MOUNTAINS AND THE GLEN OF AHERLOW

The rolling hills, flat fields, and wide ditches around Lismacue House are clarion calls to those who love a good gallop with the sun on their back.

bay gelding who responds calmly to every twitch of your thigh. Even beginners aren't nervous as your motherly guide, Annette, riding ancient Charlie, leads the way. High you climb into the rolling hills of the Galtees, where trails thick with heather snake through little woods up to isolated lakes at 3,000 feet, still and shiny as silver dimes. On your right: the fertile Glen of Aherlow, dairy heartland of greenest Ireland. To the left: the rocky Ballyhoura Mountains, grazing land of fearless, black-faced mountain sheep. Later, in your enamel claw-foot tub, you revel in the pleasure of stiffness easing away in the rose-scented water. From the kitchen below rises the aroma of a great salmon being roasted whole. Your clothes, thrown casually over the back of the antique chair, still carry the proud scent of a day less ordinary, a day in the saddle, 15 hands above the world.

In contrast to the thought-stealing rush of
the free gallop, the slow, deliberate trek allows
you the leisure to appreciate the power of
the great Galtee Mountains and the beauty
of the lush Glen of Aherlow.

The awesome, mist-shrouded cathedral and ruins atop the 200-foot-high Rock of Cashel, ancient home to the Celtic kings of Munster and center for the early Irish church, look out over a great, fertile land dedicated to that most majestic of beasts, the horse.

All the Details

Now that your appetite is whetted for an Irish Escape, it's time to tackle the nuts and bolts of trip preparation. We've broken down by region the who, what, when, and where for each escape, as well as suggesting lodging and sightseeing in the vicinity. Prices reflect the full range throughout the year. Exchange rates at press time: 0.83 punts (L0.83)/U.K.L1.5 (Northern Ireland's currency) to the U.S. dollar. Properties are open year-round, accept credit cards, and have private baths unless otherwise stated. When writing, remember to add "Republic of Ireland" or "Northern Ireland" to the address; when phoning or faxing, dial 011-353 for the Republic, 011-44 for Northern Ireland, then the number, not including the initial zero. The many Web sites mentioned should help you organize your stay. Official sites: www.irishtouristboard.com and www.discovernorthernireland.com.

There are three major airports—Dublin, Shannon (on the west coast, 25½ km [16 mi] west of Limerick), and Belfast—but the island is so small that wherever you land shouldn't be more than a few hours from your destination. From North America and the United Kingdom, Aer Lingus (tel. 800/223-6537) is the main carrier to Ireland and Northern Ireland; Continental (tel. 800/231-0856) and Delta (tel. 800/241-4141) also have regular flights to the Republic, and several carriers in London offer frequent 1½-hour flights to Belfast.

Trains in Ireland stop only at major towns, and buses can be unreliable in isolated areas, so a car is essential if you'll be touring. It's best to arrange a rental before you leave home, and if you plan to cross the border into Northern Ireland, make sure the rental insurance will cover you on both sides. July and August are the driest months and draw hordes of tourists; May, June, September, and October can also be very crowded, as can the week around St. Patrick's Day. There's a good chance of rain whichever month you choose, so less expensive off-season travel is an option, though the best festivals and other events are crowded into the summer months, when daylight can last past 10 PM. The Southeast tends to be a little drier and sunnier than the rest of the country, while the West is the wettest.

DUBLIN

Dublin is a city on a bay, following the slow curve of the shore from the Hill of Howth in the north to the Wicklow Mountains. A river divides it into Northside and Southside, different worlds—blue-collar and wild, affluent and respectable—that have long enjoyed a friendly rivalry. But the heart of the city is a few square miles in its historic center, and almost all the major sights are within an hour's walk of one another. This is a great time to visit Dublin, when you can bear witness to an ancient city in the midst of profound and exciting change. An economic boom has brought new money and vitality, and the accents and faces of Africa, Asia, and Eastern Europe add a cosmopolitan spice to the cobbled streets and hedonistic nightlife of Temple Bar, Dublin's Left Bank. But the old stuff is still the best: the Georgian elegance of Merrion Square, the Norman drama of Christ Church Cathedral, and most of all, a thick, creamy pint in a hundred-year-old bar where the only music is the rhythm of conversation and the drama needs no TV screen.

A PUB CRAWL ALONG THE RIVER LIFFEY (8–9G)
Dublin's Black Blood, p. 62

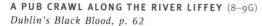

In a good pub crawl, choice of pubs is made as you go, depending on the whims of the crawlers and the quality of the Guinness on offer. Questions to ask to find an authentic old-school Dublin bar: Does it have a TV? and Was it mentioned in *Ulysses*? If the answers are no and yes, odds are you've found a good spot for a pint. It's a good idea to start at Guinness's Hop Store: The pint is pure and chilled here, and you'll still be sober enough to read and enjoy a few of the interesting exhibits. Our own tour follows the flow of the River Liffey, stopping next at the Brazen Head, the city's oldest pub, dating from 1623. Cross the river now to Ryans, home of the best "snug," or private drinking room, in Dublin.

Twilight should find you on Duke Street, where you have the choice of outdoor boozing at the upmarket Davey Byrnes or the even swisher Bailey. Night in Dublin means a visit to the Temple Bar, the eponymous red emporium of drink at the heart of Dublin's hippest district.

CONTACT Dublin Tourism, Suffolk St., just off Grafton St., Dublin 2, tel. 01/605-7799, fax 01/605-7787, www. visit-dublin.com. Guinness Hop Store, James's Gate, tel. 01/453-3645, www.guinness.com. Bailey (2 Duke St., no phone). Brazen Head (Bridge St., tel. 01/677-9549). Davey Byrnes (21 Duke St., tel. 01/671-1298). Ryans (28 Parkgate St., tel. 01/677-6097). Stag's Head (1 Dame Ct., tel. 01/679-3701). Temple Bar (48 E. Essex St., no phone).

OPTIONS If you haven't brought your own companions, you can always join an organized pub crawl (see Dublin Tourism Web site), like the **Dublin Literary Pub Crawl,** led by actors. Tel. 01/670-5602, fax 01/670-5603, www.dublinpubcrawl. com. The redbrick, Victorian **Le Meridien Shelbourne** is the perfect place to lie in late after a night on the town. Set on an elegant street with statues of Nubian princesses and slaves in the foyer, it is a bastion of old-fashioned luxury. Its Horseshoe Bar, popular with Ireland's political and business elite, serves a good Guinness in its own right. 27 St. Stephen's Green, Dublin 2, tel. 01/663-4500 or 800/543-4300, fax 01/661-6006, www.shelbourne.ie. 190 rooms, 22 suites. 2 restaurants, 2 bars, indoor pool, hot tub, sauna, health club. Double £200, suite £350. At Dublin's newest hotel, **Chief O'Neills,** rooms are minimalist, with chrome and other high-tech touches, but location is everything: It's north of the river in Smithfield Village, site of some of the finest old pubs in Dublin. Wake up early to enjoy the huge fruit and flower markets across the road. Smithfield Village, Dublin 7, tel. 01/817-3838 or 800/44-UTELL, fax 01/817-3839, www.chiefoneills.com. 69 rooms, 4 suites. Restaurant, bar, exercise room; in-room data ports, mini-bars, VCRs. Double £130, suite £295.

A GUEST HOUSE IN GEORGIAN DUBLIN (8–9G)

A Window onto an Elegant Past,
p. 24

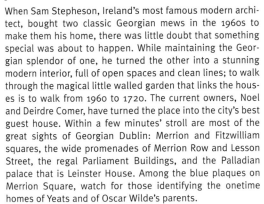

When Sam Stepheson, Ireland's most famous modern architect, bought two classic Georgian mews in the 1960s to make them his home, there was little doubt that something special was about to happen. While maintaining the Georgian splendor of one, he turned the other into a stunning modern interior, full of open spaces and clean lines; to walk through the magical little walled garden that links the houses is to walk from 1960 to 1720. The current owners, Noel and Deirdre Comer, have turned the place into the city's best guest house. Within a few minutes' stroll are most of the great sights of Georgian Dublin: Merrion and Fitzwilliam squares, the wide promenades of Merrion Row and Lesson Street, the regal Parliament Buildings, and the Palladian palace that is Leinster House. Among the blue plaques on Merrion Square, watch for those identifying the onetime homes of Yeats and of Oscar Wilde's parents.

CONTACT Number 31, 31 Lesson Close, Lower Lesson St., Dublin 2, tel. 01/676–5011, fax 01/676–2929, www.number31.ie. 21 rooms. Double £110–£180, single £70–£110, breakfast included. For neighborhood info: Irish Georgian Society, 74 Merrion Sq., Dublin 2, tel. 01/676–7073, fax 01/662–0290, www.archeire.com/igs.

OPTIONS Though larger and less personal than nearby Number 31, the **Fitzwilliam Park**, on the leafy square with a superb view of the park, has maintained much of its elegance while adding the modern conveniences. 5 Fitzwilliam Sq., Dublin 2, tel. 01/662–8280, fax 01/662–8281, www.fitzpark.ie. 20 rooms. Double £120–£130, single £95, breakfast included. **Longfields,** with its classic fanlighted front door, sits in the middle of the longest unbroken line of Georgian houses in Britain and Ireland. The rooms live up to the exterior, with curtained beds, high plastered ceilings, and floor-to-ceiling windows with patent-reveal trim. 10 Fitzwilliam St. Lower, Dublin 2, tel. 01/676–1367, fax 01/676–1542,

www.longfields.ie. 26 rooms. Double £105–£170. In Temple Bar but just a few minutes from the Georgian city is **Number 25 Eustace Street,** a 1720 town house with superb timber-paneled staircase, gloriously bright drawing room with baby grand, and full dining room. It is maintained by the Landmark Trust as a historic site, but you can rent it in its entirety. 25 Eustace St., Dublin 2, tel. 01/670–4733, fax 01/670–4887, www.irishlandmark.com. 3 bedrooms (sleep 7). £200 for 1 night to £900 for 1 week.

DUBLIN HIGHLIGHTS

The center of this 1,000-year-old city is dominated by the great walled campus of Elizabethan **Trinity College,** home to the famed Book of Kells. The twin medieval cathedrals of **Christ Church** and **St. Patrick's** are only a hundred yards apart on the south bank of the Liffey. Austere **Dublin Castle**—for generations the seat of British power in Ireland—now houses the **Chester Beatty Library,** with one of the most significant collections of Islamic and Far Eastern art in the Western world. For the "Dublin buzz," stroll down brick-lined, boutique-crammed **Grafton Street** toward a surprisingly serene park called **St. Stephen's Green.** The **Dublin Writers Museum** is a great place to begin a literary tour, perhaps following Joyce's Leopold Bloom on his one-day voyage around the city he called his "dear, dirty dumpling."

ANTRIM AND DERRY, NORTHERN IRELAND

During all the years of Northern Ireland's Troubles the landscape stood waiting. The lush valleys were quiet, the velvety beaches empty, and rivers teeming with silver salmon and brown trout flowed without interruption. But this time of peace has brought new life to Antrim and Derry as visitors discover their relatively untapped treasures. The region is steeped in the mythology of the Ulster cycle, tales of a time when the great Celtic heroes like Cuchulainn skipped across the age-old natural wonder of the Giant's Causeway, on the north coast, and

swam Lough Neagh, Britain's largest lake. You can almost see them bestriding the Glens of Antrim, a mini-Switzerland of peaks, valleys, and waterfalls a stone's throw from the coves and bays of the sea.

A DRIVE ALONG THE ANTRIM COAST THROUGH THE GLENS (7–8A–B)
Over Hill and Dale, p. 64

Ireland's famous coastline has become crowded over the last decade, so the relatively undiscovered Antrim Coast is a treat. It's great driving country, with scenic roads narrow and meandering enough to keep you interested but well-maintained enough to make it safe. The near legendary courtesy of Irish country drivers adds to the pleasure. The plenitude of little towns scattered through the Glens—nine valleys converging on the open sea within a few miles of each other—ensures that you'll never go hungry or thirsty, and interaction with the locals, who have not met enough tourists to be sick of them, is usually filled with humor and warmth. If you just have to get out of the car for a day and do some serious walking, Glenariff Forest Park (8B), in the largest of the Glens, has dozens of quality hikes, notably the 5½ km (3½ mi) Waterfall Trail down the Glenariff River and its dizzying number of waterfalls to a small lough perfect for a dip.

CONTACT Northern Ireland Tourist Board, Donegal Sq., Belfast, tel. 048/9024–6609, fax 048/9031–2424, www.discovernorthernireland.com.

DISTANCES The drive: 74 km (46 mi) from Carnlough in the south to Ballintoy in the north. Carnlough is 24 km (15 mi) north of the port of Larne and 64 km (40 mi) northeast of Belfast.

OPTIONS A classic seaside town must have an elegant old lady of a hotel. Carnlough (8B) has the ivy-covered **Londonderry Arms,** built in 1848 as a coach house by Lady Londonderry, inherited by her grandson, Winston Churchill,

and bought by the O'Neill family in 1946. With its Georgian architecture still intact, a piano lounge where locals like to sing old romantic ballads, and the best pint of stout in the North, it is the place of choice for discerning travelers in these parts. The restaurant offers the freshest seafood and local produce. 20 Harbour Rd., Carnlough, Co. Antrim, BT44 0EU, tel. 048/2888–5255, fax 048/2888–5263, www.glensofantrim.com. 35 rooms. Bar. Double £85, single £55. Among the myriad tea shops that dot the Glens, **Roarke's Kitchen** (tel. 048/207–63632)—owned by the Roarkes, shipwrecked in Ballintoy (7A) a couple centuries back—"steals the biscuit."

FLY FISHING THE RIVERS BANN AND AGIVEY (6–7B)
Dance of the Fly, p. 70

The eternal questions of game fishing are when, where, and with what bait. In the rivers of Northern Ireland the answers usually lie in the head of your ghillie. They're a pleasure to spend the day with, having mastered the art of when to speak and when to stay silent. The Lower Bann is the North's biggest river, flowing out of Lough Neagh into the North Channel. Its levels are controlled by man, and it is stocked with salmon and brown trout. A number of ghillies compete for work at the prime spot of Carnroe, so they tend to be brash, funny men never short of a good yarn. The Agivey—a David to the Bann's Goliath—is actually a tributary of the larger river, rented out to the fishing club of the town of Agivey (7B). Angling here is at an altogether gentle pace, and the ghillies who work this river are patient, country men. Gear and licenses can be arranged through your guide or at Bert's tackle shop in Garvagh (6B).

CONTACT Fishing licenses are available directly from Edward Montgomery at Bann System Ltd. (tel. 048/7034–4796), which owns the rights to the Lower Bann. The main ghillies on the Bann are Robbie Moffet (tel. 078/0118–5588), Harry Patten (tel. 077/1494–9103), and Ray Corr (tel. 077/3021–8711). To fish the Agivey, the world calls Bert

Atkins (shop: 67 Coleraine Rd., Garvagh, Co. Derry, BT51 5HR, tel. 048/2955–7691, fax 048/2955–7692).

DISTANCES Agivey village is 10 km (6 mi) south of Coleraine, 50 km (31 mi) east of Derry City.

PRICES The price of a license to fish the Bann varies with the season and the number in your party, but expect to pay up to U.K.£300 for a day; half-day rates are available. The Agivey costs as little as U.K.£15 for a day. Guides' fees are negotiated, depending on size of party and time of year.

OPTIONS Bill O'Hara, the most gregarious host you could wish for, and his family have owned the **Brown Trout Golf & Country Inn** for more than 300 years. Anglers gather at the great oak bar after eating local fish and fauna in the hearty restaurant. 209 Agivey Rd., Aghadowey BT51 4AD, Co. Derry, tel. 048/7086–8209, fax 048/7086–8878, www.browntroutinn. com. 18 rooms, 3 cottages. 9-hole golf course. Double £60–£85, single £45–£57.50; cottage £300 for 3-day-minimum stay. The **Moorbrook Lodge,** on five unspoiled acres overlooking its own well-stocked trout lake, offers a fire-warmed drawing room and simple, bright rooms with glorious views to the coast and over the sea to Scotland. 46 Glebe Rd., Castlerock, Coleraine BT51 4SW, Co. Derry, tel./fax 048/7084–9408, www.moorbrooklodge.freeserve.co.uk. 4 rooms. Trout lake, alternative therapies (reflexology, massage, etc.). Double £50, breakfast included.

MASTERING THE LINKS OF NORTHERN IRELAND (6A–B)
Tee and Sympathy, p. 34

Thirty-nine of the world's top 150 links are in Ireland, and some of the best and most scenic (as well as most underused) are in Northern Ireland, which *Golf Digest* ranks as the No. 4 golf destination in the world. Royal Portrush is the only club outside England and Scotland to have held a British Open. The 425-yard, par-4 first at the humbler, century-old Portstewart is infamously difficult, as it falls away from a great height to a tiny green between two dunes. Both clubs are private, but visitors are welcome. Both have older, less-

trying courses if you get tired of searching for balls in the championship courses' tall grass. But perhaps the greatest thing about the courses is their location, at the end of the Antrim Coast drive (see "Over Hill and Dale," p. 64).

CONTACT Royal Portrush, Dunluce Rd., Portrush BT56 8JQ, Co. Antrim, tel. 048/7082–2311. Portstewart Golf Club, 117 Strand Rd., Portstewart BT55 7PT, Co. Derry, tel. 048/7083–2015.

DISTANCES Royal Portrush is 88 km (55 mi) northwest of Belfast, Portstewart a few miles farther west down the coast road.

PRICES Royal Portrush: weekdays U.K.£60, weekends U.K.£70. Portstewart: weekdays U.K.£45, weekends U.K.£65.

OPTIONS Royal County Down (8D) is considered the toughest course in Northern Ireland (watch out for bunkers the size of craters), and one of the most beautiful. Golf Links Rd., Newcastle BT33 0AN, Co. Down, tel. 048/4372–2419. The idyllic, relatively benign course at **Ballycastle Golf** (7A) is built around the ruins of a 13th-century abbey. 2 Cushendall Rd., Ballycastle BT54 6QP, Co. Antrim, tel. 048/2076–2536. The historic feel of the **Bushmills Inn** (6A), an old coaching inn, is preserved in open peat fires, pine furnishings, gas lights, and small, very cozy bedrooms; the old livery stables are now a favorite local restaurant. 9 Dunluce Rd., Bushmills BT57 8QG, Co. Antrim, tel. 048/2073–2339, fax 048/2073–2048, www.bushmills-inn.com. Restaurant, bar. 32 rooms. Double £118–£128, single £58–£68.

ANTRIM AND DERRY HIGHLIGHTS
Belfast (8C) is a grimy, busy city only the Victorians could build. The Golden Mile, an arrow-shaped area from Howard Street to Shaftesbury Square, includes such architectural pleasures as the 1898 City Hall, the Far Eastern–inspired Grand Opera House, and the city's most famous pub, the richly decorated Crown Liquor Saloon. On the shore of Belfast Lough, **Carrickfergus** (8C) is an ancient town famous for its 12th-century castle. The **Giant's Causeway** (7A), Northern Ireland's premier tourist attraction, consists of

40,000 pillars of volcanic basalt—some 40 feet high—extending out from the Antrim Coast into the sea. **Derry** (5B) is Northern Ireland's second city, and its most historic. Much of the medieval walls still stands, and the Tower Museum, chronicling the history of Derry, is inside a reconstructed tower set into them. Free Derry Corner is a white gable wall where nationalists painted slogans opposing British rule in the North; elsewhere giant nationalist and loyalist wall murals celebrate various heroes. The small town of **Bushmills** (6A) is home to the oldest licensed distillery in the world (1608).

THE NORTHWEST: DONEGAL AND SLIGO

Always last to be conquered, farthest from the seat of power, the Northwest has gone its own, rugged way. The people are different here than in the rest of Ireland, wilder, a little more free. They even look different, with raven-dark hair and milk-white skin, the tones of the old Celts, untouched by Norseman and Norman alike. The most northerly part of Ireland's Atlantic coastline runs from Sligo along Donegal's remote, windy peninsulas to Malin Head (5A) in the far north. Donegal was part of the ancient kingdom of Ulster, where the legendary Cuchulainn was the champion of king and people alike. Today it is Ireland's largest Gaeltacht, or Irish-speaking region. It is a land where mountains fall suddenly away to the sea, providing spectacular vistas and meandering drives along narrow roads. The many beaches are a treat, with deep white sand, magenta water, and only a few people enjoying the glory of it all. Sligo Town is undergoing something of a renaissance, with little bookshops, cafés, and galleries springing up on its winding streets. The surrounding countryside can seem bleak, but it is the very heart of ancient Ireland, still relatively untamed by modern development, broken up by little villages where to this day sheep and cattle going to market have the right of way.

A COTTAGE STAY IN THE LAND OF DONEGAL TWEED (3–4C)
Weaving the Elements, p. 54

Ardara has long been the hub of Donegal tweed, with home weavers fanning out for 4 miles around. Early this century, when there were more than 300 weavers, the men and their dogs would bring down the mountain sheep and shear them in June, the women would card and spin the wool, then the men would weave the cloth and sell it. Alas, it is now an old man's art. Take the time to stroll around and visit a few of the weavers who remain. They tend to live in some of the most isolated and beautiful spots, and they are usually men with stories to tell. Peter McGuire is a prince among them, and a stay in the little cottage he rents drops you right into the heart of the community. Ardara itself, and larger Donegal Town to the south, are meccas for tweed shoppers, with the best prices and selection in the known world.

CONTACT The Ardara Heritage Centre (Main St., Ardara, tel. 075/41262), tourist office for the region, has a museum dedicated to weaving and a working loom and weaver. It can put you in touch with the local weavers. Useful site: www.ardara.ie.

DISTANCES 40 km (25 mi) northwest of Donegal Town

OPTIONS McGuire's **Curragh Mor Cottage** has two big bedrooms, a parlor, and a huge kitchen. Carrickatcleave, Ardara, tel. 075/41413. Weekly: £250 July–Aug., £150 June and Sept., £100 Oct.–May. Off-season holiday weekend: £75. The town has a number of fine B&Bs, but the hospitality and humor of Eileen Molloy and the turf fire in the lounge overlooking mountains and sea make the **Greenhaven** a cut above the rest. Portnoo Rd., Ardara, tel./fax 075/41129. 6 rooms. Double £38, single £19. No credit cards. Closed Dec. **Francis O'Donnell** is another weaver who loves visitors. A lively, opinionated man, he will tell you a great deal about the history of the craft in the area (he almost spits the words "power loom"). 173 Ardconnell, Ardara, tel. 075/41688. Of the tweed shops that line Ardara's main street, **Connell Kennedy's** (tel. 075/41381) has the best selection and prices, as well as great chunky sweaters. **Nancy's** on the main street (tel. 075/41187), a little white-washed pub with rows of ugly mugs hanging over the bar, is famous hereabouts for its ultrafresh seafood, perfect pints, and chowder not of this world.

COUNTY SLIGO: YEATS COUNTRY (3–4E)
In the Poet's Footsteps, p. 50

Remote from all the major cities, wild, mysterious Sligo drew poets and writers of Ireland's late 19th-century Celtic revival to the region, and Yeats's brother Jack memorialized its landscapes in his paintings. It is an area best discovered on foot, a copy of the poet's works in your backpack. As you arrive at each sight—the view of Ben Bulben's flat peak, the pools and waterfalls of Glencar Lough, the Georgian mansion Lissadell, where he visited friends—pluck the tome from your bag and let his words illuminate your surroundings. (There's also a signposted Yeats trail around Lough Gill.) Yeats was a man of means, and when he stayed in the country, he did so in style; you can too by sampling the many Sligo stately homes now operating as guest houses.

CONTACT The Yeats Memorial Building has information on all Yeats-related sights and events in the area. Hyde Bridge, Sligo Town, tel. 071/45847. Drumcliffe Visitors Centre, tel. 071/44956, fax 071/63125, www.drumcliffe.ie. Useful sites: www.yeats-sligo.com, www.sligo.ie.

DISTANCES Sligo Town is 138 km (986 mi) northeast of Galway, 217 km (135 mi) northwest of Dublin.

OPTIONS Seven generations of O'Haras have lived in the splendid three-story Georgian farmhouse **Coopershill.** You'll wallow in the beautiful antique-furnished rooms with four-poster beds, and the century-old enamel bath and shower. Every room has a view of the grounds, with woods and deer farm. Dinner is served by candlelight. Riverstown, Co. Sligo, tel. 071/65108, fax 071/65466, www.coopers

hill.com. 8 rooms. Tennis court, croquet lawn, boating, fishing. Double £112–£126, single £66–£73, breakfast included. Closed Nov.–mid-Mar. **Cromleach Lodge,** a modern building on a hillside whose every window seems to overlook Lough Arrow, has a country-house feel and a restaurant specializing in seafood. Castlebaldwin, Co. Sligo, tel. 071/65155, fax 071/65455, www.cromleach.com. 10 rooms. Bar, fishing. Double £150–£210, single £105–£135, breakfast included. Closed Nov.–Jan. The first two weeks of August, the Yeats Memorial Building in Sligo (see Contact) runs the **Yeats International Summer School** (tel. 071/42693; also see www.yeats-sligo.com). Lovers of the poet come from all over the world to attend lectures and readings, go on field trips, and get drunk while reciting their favorite lines.

THE NORTHWEST HIGHLIGHTS
In **Sligo Town** (4E), the Niland Gallery houses one of the country's major collections of contemporary Irish art, and St. John's Cathedral is a fine example of Georgian church design, with its elegant square tower and fortifications. The Donegal coast makes for a great driving tour; the 3½ km (2 mi) long beach of picturesque **Mullaghmore** (4D) and the busy fishing village of **Killybegs** (3D) are two favorite stops. In **Donegal Town** (4D), visit the historic castle and the nearby Franciscan Abbey, impressively situated above the Eske River as it widens into Donegal Bay. Locals argue that the **Slieve League Cliffs** (3D) beat out the famous Cliffs of Moher. The House of St. Columba, on the cliff rising north of the tiny hamlet of **Glencolumbkille** (3C), is one of Ireland's oldest pilgrimage sites. The tidy seaside village of **Dunfanaghy** (4B) is the perfect base from which to explore northern Donegal. **Horn Head** (4B), with cliffs rising 600 feet, is the most spectacular of the county's many headlands. An hour's boat ride will take you to **Tory Island** (4B), whose ruins prove it's been continuously inhabited since prehistoric times.

THE WEST

"The West's awake!" goes the old battle cry, and these days Ireland's previously neglected western counties of Clare, Galway, and Mayo are indeed in the middle of a renaissance of sorts. Vibrant Galway is, in fact, Ireland's fastest-growing city. A splendid mishmash of sheep-strewn mountains, great, still lakes, and froth-battered coastline, the West is elemental Ireland, rich with traces of the prehistoric past: the moonscape of the Burren, the mysterious Aran Islands, the glacial lakes of Connemara. "To Hell or to Connaught" was Cromwell's ultimatum to the native Irish, and many fled west to preserve their religion and their traditions. Today 40,000 native Irish speakers make their home here. Every pub worth the name will echo at night to the sound of pipe, flute, and fiddle as traditional musicians stir up the cauldron of the heart.

FLEADH NUA, IRISH MUSIC FESTIVAL AT ENNIS, COUNTY CLARE (3-41-J)
The Music of Ancients, p. 36

For nearly 30 years the Fleadh Nua ("new festival") at Ennis has been one of the premier gatherings of traditional musicians in the country. There's a full plate of concerts, master classes, and lectures, but the real action takes place in the bars, where impromptu gatherings ("sessions") of musicians lead to wild nights of revelry. Many of the finest Irish dancers also gather, and if the weather is good, you'll be treated to the sight and sound of scores of girls and boys in almost tropically bright costumes dancing in the cobblestone streets and lanes. Another favorite performance is that of the *seanachaí*, or storyteller. Expect to be amazed, terrified, and amused in turn by tales of fairies, ghosts, and heroes by Eddie Lenihan, master in the art of the yarn. Admission to all events is £20.

CONTACT Fleadh Nua Office, Tourist Information Centre, 54 O'Connell St., Ennis, Co. Clare, tel. 065/684-2988, fax 065/682-4783, www.fleadhnua.com.

DISTANCES 37 km (23 mi) northwest of Limerick, 138 km (86 mi) north of Tralee

OPTIONS In the center of Ennis, the **Old Ground Hotel** is a classic Irish small-town hotel with small, clean rooms. The real draw is the music and dance that goes on in its pub all day every day during the *fleadh* (pronounced "flah"). After a "skinful of pints" and a night of jigging and reeling, it's nice to have your bed so near. O'Connell St., Ennis, Co. Clare, tel. 065/682-8127, fax 065/682-8112, oldground.ennis.ie. 85 rooms. Double £70-£120, single £60-£80, suite £110-£140, breakfast included. Closed Dec. 24-25. The town can fill up quickly during the festival, and you might find it a bit too hectic anyway, so nearby **Carnelly House** is the perfect option. This redbrick, 250-year-old Queen Anne is full of extravagant plasterwork and stunning antiques, and every room has views out over the pastoral 90-acre estate. The restaurant is renowned for its game and fish dishes. Clarecastle, Co. Clare, tel. 065/682-8442, fax 065/682-9222. 5 rooms. Horseback riding, fishing. Double £180, single £160. Closed Dec.-Jan. Qualifiers from the country's many fleadhs compete in the Fleadh Cheoil na hEireann, the **All-Ireland Music Festival**; 10,000 players usually show up, and 4,000 compete. The location changes each year (www.comhaltas.com).

THE BURREN, COUNTY CLARE (3-4I)
Walking on the Moon, p. 58

The stark geologic anomaly called the Burren covers 300 sq km (116 sq mi), following the coast from Kinvara in the north to Doolin and the breathtaking Cliffs of Moher in the south. Though it seems a barren wasteland, it is in fact a botanist's playground, an intriguing mix of rare flora from vastly different climatic zones having taken root in the shallow earth between the cracks in the stone carpet. A visit to the Burren Display Centre can help orient you to the animal and plant life in the area, but the best way to see the Burren is with a local guide, and Shane Conolly is the wisest of the wise when it comes to this giant rock garden on Ireland's Atlantic coast.

CONTACT Reach Conolly through the Tourist Information Offices at the Cliffs of Moher (open only in summer, tel. 065/708–1171) and in Ennis: 54 O'Connell St., Ennis, Co. Clare, tel. 065/684–2988, fax 065/682–4783.

OPTIONS Near the fishing village of Ballyvaughan (3l)—a great spot for Irish music—the Haden family has long run **Gregans Castle,** a Victorian country house with homey touches like vases of wildflowers and a huge turf fire in the bar. The bedrooms, furnished with antiques and William Morris wallpapers, overlook the English gardens below, with Galway Bay and the Burren in the distance. Ballyvaughan, Co. Clare, tel. 065/707–7005, fax 065/707–7111, www.gregans.ie. 18 rooms. Award-winning restaurant. Double £146–£198, single £126–£178, suite £250–£290, breakfast included. Closed late Oct.–Mar. At **Hyland's Hotel,** a family-run 18th-century coaching inn, the smell of a turf fire greets you in the lobby, and music can usually be heard coming from the little bar. Rooms can be small but are all brightly decorated and full of light. Ask for one with a Burren view. Ballyvaughan, Co. Clare, tel. 065/707–7037, fax 065/707–7131. 30 rooms. Restaurant. Double £93, single £60. Closed Dec.–Jan. Ennis (see "Fleadh Nua...," p.87) is a pleasant town to stay in if you're touring the Burren. Mary and Denis O'Callaghan's sprawling Victorian lodge, **Ballinalacken Castle**, sits atop a hill just outside the town of Lisdoonvarna. Views to the west are of the Aran Islands and the Connemara Mountains; to the east lie 100 acres of wildflower meadows. Rooms come in all sizes; try to get one with a marble fireplace and high ceilings. Lisdoonvarna, Co. Clare, tel. 065/707–4025, fax 065/707–4025, e-mail to ballinalackencastle@eircom.net. 12 rooms. Restaurant, bar. Double £70–£90, single £50. Closed Oct.–Mar.

THE REGATTA AT KINVARA, COUNTY GALWAY (3l)
Gathering of the Boats, p. 40

Two main types of boats take part in the Cruinniú na mBád, is held place the second weekend in August: the hookers, particular to the Irish coast, and the currachs, wickerwork rowing boats covered with hide. The currach races, with crews of two, four, and more, are enthralling tests of strength, with decades-old rivalries on display. You'll hear a lot of Irish spoken over the weekend, as many of the visitors are down from the Gaeltachts of Galway and Clare. Every bar will be packed and alive with excited talk of the day's races. Foreign visitors are in the minority, but you can expect a warm welcome. Though it gets its share of tourists, Kinvara has managed to stay Irish and western. It is a lively place throughout the summer, with traditional music sessions in most bars every weekend and the Cuckoo Fleadh on the first weekend in May starting things off with traditional music and arts and wild parties.

CONTACT Tourist Information Office, Victoria Pl., Eyre Sq., Galway, Co. Galway, tel. 091/563–081, fax 091/565–201. Useful site: www.kinvara.com.

DISTANCES 25 km (15½ mi) south of Galway City

OPTIONS The whitewashed, thatched **Merriman Inn,** on the shores of the bay, manages to combine a picturesque exterior with the interior of a modern hotel. The rooms are nothing special, but try to get one looking out onto the water. The bar and lounge have great open fires where guests and locals gather. Local seafood, including lobster, is the specialty of the restaurant. Main St., Kinvara, Co. Galway, tel. 091/638–222, fax 091/637–686, www.merrimanhotel.com. 32 rooms. Double £65–£85, single £45–£55, breakfast included. Closed Jan. On the edge of the bay with magnificent views of the Burren and green fields lies the **Burren View Farm,** a B&B on a working sheep farm. The rooms are simple but spotless, and the pub is a short walk away. Doorus, Kinvara, Co. Galway, tel. 091/637–142, fax 091/638–131. 5 rooms, 2 with bath. Tennis court, fishing, meals on request. Double £60, single £40. Closed Nov.–Feb.

INIS MÓR, ARAN ISLANDS (2I)
An Island That Time Forgot, p. 18

The Aran Islands—Inis Mór ("big island," pop. 900), Inis Meáin ("middle island," pop. 300), and Inis Óirr ("eastern island," pop. 250)—constitute the westernmost outpost of the ancient kingdom of Connaught. They are cut from the same chunk of moonlike limestone as the Burren, and the two landscapes have many similarities. But the Aran Islands have been inhabited at least since the Iron Age. Scattered around are numerous pre-Christian forts and monuments, real archaeological treasures around which you're free to roam. There are also fine examples of early churches and Christian graveyards. The islands' isolation allowed Celtic culture to survive while it was under attack on the mainland. This is most obvious in the widespread use of Irish and in the wearing of the traditional white Aran sweater. The islands' elemental nature has attracted artists for years. The playwright J. M. Synge based many of his works on time spent here, and the American Robert Flaherty's *Man of Aran* was a major film in 1934. The best time to visit is June or August, when the rugged landscape is overrun with red clover, daisies, saxifrage, and harebells.

CONTACT Aran Island Tourist Office, Kilronan, Inis Mór, tel. 099/61263; open mid-Mar.–Oct. 5. Galway Tourist Information Office, Victoria Pl., Eyre Sq., Galway, Co. Galway, tel. 091/563–081, fax 091/565–201. For 15-minute flights from Connemara Airport: Aer Arann, tel. 091/593–034, www.aer-arann.ie. For 60- to 90-minute ferry trips from Rossaveel in Connemara, Galway City, or Doolin in County Clare (as well as other useful info), see www.aran-islands.com.

DISTANCES 48 km (30 mi) by boat from Galway City

OPTIONS Kilmurvey House, an 18th-century stone farmhouse near Inis Mór's second village, Bun Gowla, is right beside a beautiful sandy beach perfect for swimming (if you don't mind a bit of cold water). Treasa Joyce and her mother, Brigid, run a relaxed ship, and they're always willing to offer advice. The gargantuan feasts they serve most evenings are a joy. Bun Gowla, Inis Mór, Co. Galway, tel. 099/61218, fax 099/61397, e-mail: kilmurveyhouse@tinet.ie. 12 rooms. Double £50, single £30, breakfast included. The family-run guesthouse **Tigh Fitz** is in the hamlet of Killeany, next to the beach and not far from the cliffs. Killeany, Kilronan, Inis Mór, Co. Galway, tel. 099/61189 or 099/61213, fax 099/61386. 11 rooms. Pub. Double £50, single £30, breakfast included.

BIKING THROUGH THE HILLS OF CONNEMARA (1–3G–I)
The Agony and the Ecstasy, p. 20

A number of groups organize cycling trips through the heartland of Connemara, but Bike Riders' is the most comprehensive and well run. The key to its success is its guides, who tend to be professional, humorous, and lovers of shooting the breeze over long dinners. Irish Johnny and American Mims are the cream of the crop. You start in the Burren in County Clare; head up through Ballyvaughan (3I) to the Cliffs of Moher (3I); cycle from the ruined abbey at Cong (3G) by Lough Nafooey and into Leenane (2G); ride the famous Sky Road into the mountains of Connemara through isolated communities and into Clifden (1H), a town synonymous with Irish traditional music; and wheel through peat bogs into Irish-speaking areas like Roundstone (1H) and Cashel (2H). Along the way there's shopping in Galway City, a stopover on an island where St. Patrick lived, and a day of options (a visit to remote Inishbofin [1G], a tiny island with medieval ruins and a great cycling path around its edge; a day of golf; or a visit to the Irish crafts center at Kylemore Abbey [1H]). At the end of a hard day in the saddle you'll revel in the luxury of accommodations like the 17th-century Gregans Castle in the Burren, the flashy Great Southern Hotel in Galway, and the Rosleague Manor in Connemara.

CONTACT Bike Riders Tours, Box 130254, Boston, MA 02113, tel. 617/723–2354 or 800/473–7040, fax 617/723–2355, www.bikeriderstours.com. Useful site: www.connemara-tourism.org.

PRICES The eight-day "Ireland's Western Shore" tour, offered June–Sept., costs $2,580 per person, including everything but rental of a 24-speed bike ($150).

OPTIONS If you prefer a more flexible itinerary, it's easy to set up your own trip in the West. You can bring your own bike—airlines accept them as part of your check-in luggage—or rent one (and other equipment) in any major town in the region for about £8 a day or £40 a week. **Raleigh Ireland** runs an organized rental, repair, and drop-off service out of bike shops throughout the country. Raleigh House, Kylemore Rd., Dublin 10, tel. 01/626–1333.

THE WEST HIGHLIGHTS
One of Ireland's most spectacular sights, the soft shale and sandstone **Cliffs of Moher** (3I) rise 710 feet out of the crashing Atlantic. Different rock strata are visible in the cliff face, and a brave colony of puffins has chosen the shelves in the rock as their nesting place. From atop O'Briens Tower, at the cliffs' highest point, you can see the Aran Islands, the mountains of Kerry, and the wild hills of Connemara. The nearby town of **Doolin** (3I) has become very popular with visitors because of its music pubs, which draw European and Irish folk musicians. The two smaller Aran Islands get fewer visitors and are even more unspoiled and small enough to explore on foot; **Inis Meáin** (2I) has Conor Fort, a smaller version of Dún Aengus, plus the ruins of two early Christian churches. In 18th-century **Westport** (2G), one of the prettiest towns in Ireland, all the streets radiate from its central Octagon, site of a weekly, old-fashioned farmer's market; about a mile outside town is stately, Georgian Westport House. No tour of the West would be complete without a visit to Ireland's most exciting city, **Galway** (3H). Bustling Eyre Square, with a hodgepodge of monuments, is the geographic and cultural heart of Galway. Other noteworthy sites are the 16th-century fortified house Lynch's Castle and the elegant 1584 Spanish Arch, a reminder of past links with Spain.

THE MIDLANDS
The extremely fertile Midlands is the country's most overlooked region—a plus for the adventurous traveler. In Ireland's sea of green, it is awash with islands of crystal clear blue: A fair share of the country's 800 bodies of water speckle this lush countryside. The relatively flat lands to the north rise a little to become the Galtee Mountains of Tipperary. The area around the picturesque Golden Vale and the ancient Rock of Cashel has perhaps more quality equine bloodstock per square foot than any other on the planet. The many affluent market towns like Athlone (5G) and Roscrea (6I) offer an opportunity to observe the Irish going about their everyday lives, unaffected by the relatively few tourists walking among them.

A BARGE TRIP ON THE SHANNON (5G–J)
Queen of the River, p. 28

The lordly Shannon runs 259 km (162 mi) right through the heartland of Ireland, from its source in County Cavan's Cuilcagh Mountains (5E) down through the Midlands before emptying into the great estuary near Limerick City (4J). The 12-passenger *Shannon Princess* travels the most scenic part of the waterway. It is also a great part of the country for wildlife, so bring binoculars to catch kingfishers buzzing around wild orchids and birds of prey hunting salmon headed upstream. Each day you stop off to wander bustling little towns like Terryglass (5I) and Banagher (5H), explore historic sites like Portumna Castle and the monastery ruins at Clonmacnoise, and visit Galway City. Side trips for fishing, hunting, or shopping can be arranged.

CONTACT *Shannon Princess*, Lakeside Marina, Ballykeeran, Athlone, Co. Westmeath, tel. 087/251–4807, fax 087/201–1022, e-mail: ireland@greenbook.ie.

PRICES $2,290 per person, including all meals, alcohol, shore excursions, and taxes.

OPTIONS You can rent a boat with some friends and crew it yourself. Boat holidays in Ireland are becoming ever more popular, and there's usually a great camaraderie among crews. The only problem? Everyone wants to be skipper, and no one wants to be cook. **Celtic Canal Cruisers** gives you a lesson in how to steer your two- to nine-berth rental and sends you on your way with a map. Tullamore, Co. Offaly, tel. 0506/21861, fax 0506/51266, www.celticcanalcruisers.com. Sample prices (with seasonal variations): 2 berths, £331–£552; 9 berths, £760–£1,267.

RIDING IN THE GALTEE MOUNTAINS AND THE GLEN OF AHERLOW (5–6J–K)
Life in the Saddle, p. 72

When you talk about horses in horse-mad Ireland, two areas come to mind: County Kildare, around the Curragh, and emerald green south Tipperary. The Galtee Mountains area is home to the country's finest hunts, some of its major studs, and a number of its top racehorse trainers. But folks here aren't snobby about it—practically every farmer and his wife ride, competitively or just for pleasure. The rolling hills, flat fields with wide ditches, gently rising mountain trails, and fast forest paths are made for a leisurely trot or a carefree canter. Lismacue has the dizzyingly high ceilings, intricate plasterwork, and grand staircases of a grand country house but none of the stuffiness, thanks to the family, as laid-back and convivial as any B&B proprietors. At dinner, Jim's urbane but gentle wit and French-trained Kate's blue-ribbon cooking are twin delights.

CONTACT Lismacue House, Bansha, Co. Tipperary, tel. 062/54106, fax 062/54126, e-mail: lismac@indigo.ie. 5 rooms, 3 with bath. Dining room, trout fishing, stables. Double £110, single £66. Closed Dec. 22–Jan. 2.

DISTANCES 9½ km (6 mi) from Tipperary Town

OPTIONS Hillcrest School of Equestrian Activities, another family-run operation, is the best in the area for trekking, from day rides with picnic lunch to a six-day post-to-post ride on the Ballyhoura Mountains trail. A challenging cross-country course, show jumping instruction, and hunting holidays are offered. Galbally, Co. Limerick, tel./fax 062/37915, www.irishabroad.com/travel/horseriding/hillcrest/offer.htm. The **Cashel Palace Hotel,** dramatically located at the foot of the Rock of Cashel, was built in 1730 as an archbishop's palace. Rooms are luxurious, with huge bathrooms; period furnishings, marble fireplaces, and a great winding staircase add to the splendor. The restaurant, with views onto the gardens, concentrates on game and local produce. Main St., Cashel, Co. Tipperary, tel. 062/62707, fax 062/61521, www.cashel-palace.ie. 23 rooms. Bar, fishing. Double £225, single £150. On arrival at **The Grove,** a snug B&B in Cashel Town, you'll be welcomed with a cup of tea and homemade scones or banana bread. Rooms are spacious and full of light, and historic sites are in walking distance. R688, Cashel, Co. Tipperary, tel. 062/62382. 4 rooms. Double £40, single £25. Closed mid-Oct.–Easter.

THE BALLINASLOE HORSE FAIR AND SHOW (5H)
The Farmers' Holiday, p. 8

Though officially in east County Galway, the market town of Ballinasloe is nearer to Athlone than to Galway City, more part of Ireland's midland plain than of the rugged, mountainous west. The horse fair, held at the beginning of October, has long been one of the biggest in the world. Mounts for the Russian cavalry as well as Napoleon were once purchased here. For the visitor, the weeklong event is a golden opportunity to observe the peasant farmer, who shaped the nation, in his natural habitat—and to share in the socializing. Every bar in town is packed to the rafters, and few are without music. A parade of vintage farm equipment and a ferocious tug-of-war bring the crowds out onto the street. Tourists tend to be thin on the ground, but you'll be welcomed. Most of the sellers in the field are members of Ireland's gypsylike community known as travellers; extended families gather every year at the fair and ensure that the party never dies down.

CONTACT Ballinasloe Horse Fair and Show, Ballinasloe, Co.

Galway, tel. 0905/43453, fax 0905/44132, www. ballinasloe.com.

DISTANCES 64 km (40 mi) from Galway, 144 km (90 mi) from Dublin

OPTIONS If you want to capture the full flavor and excitement of the fair experience, **Hayden's Gateway Hotel** is the only place to stay. The floors of the foyer and bar are covered with plastic for the week in anticipation of all the mucky boots and beer-spilling mayhem. Otherwise, the place is unexciting, with modern pine-and-pastels decor and good-size bedrooms. Ballinasloe, Co. Galway, tel. 065/682–3000, fax 065/682–3759, www.lynchotels.com. Restaurant, nightclub. 48 rooms. Double £86–£118, breakfast included. For a more peaceful stay, head a little out of town to **Flowerhill House**, a Georgian country house that's part of a 250-acre equestrian center. Oliver Walsh, the gregarious and helpful owner, has big antique-furnished rooms, some with three beds. The gorgeous grounds are full of horses; trail rides, cross-country, hunting, trekking, and show jumping are offered. The dining room serves quality local produce. Killimore, Ballinasloe, Co. Galway, tel. 0905/76112, fax 0905/76462, www.flowerhill.net. 10 rooms. Double £36, breakfast included.

MIDLANDS HIGHLIGHTS
The most popular site in the region is the awe-inspiring **Rock of Cashel** (6J), for centuries the seat of kings; a monastery and church were later built atop the 200-ft-high rock. The 6th-century monastery of **Clonmacnoise** (5H) is early Christian Ireland's most important and impressive site; its Celtic high cross and round tower are nonpareil. The Irish Palladian wonder **Emo Court and Gardens** (7H), in County Laois, is typical of a style of grand country house that dots the region; other examples are Strokestown Park House in County Roscommon and Tullynally Castle and Gardens in County Westmeath. Much of the Midlands is bogland, and the **Bord Na Mona Bog Rail Tour** (near Shannonbridge [5H], tel. 0905/74114) by narrow-gauge railway is a unique way to survey this strange, marshy landscape. **Lough Key Forest Park** (4F), with a deer enclosure and a cypress grove, is 840 acres of unspoiled woods on the banks of a peaceful lake near Boyle.

THE SOUTHWEST
The large, mountainous counties of Cork and Kerry, with their spectacular coastline and varied landscape, make up Ireland's legendary Southwest. With the Lakes of Killarney, the Ring of Kerry, and the Dingle Peninsula as the prime attractions, tourist buses long ago discovered the wonder of the area. But somehow, especially in West Cork, the best of the secret places remain hidden. Miles of winding country roads pass by rich pastureland rising to rocky limestone peaks that sweep suddenly down to the Atlantic. These counties suffered worse than most in the centuries of occupation—Cork to this day is known as "the rebel county"—and especially during the black years of the famine. As a result, the spirit of Celtic Ireland is still strong here, with Irish the main language in many rural areas. The locals are famed for their gentle wit and informal hospitality, making this a great place for a stay at a country house or B&B. And nowhere will you see the vibrancy of the Irish landscape better displayed in its infinite variety of greens and golds.

BANTRY HOUSE AND THE BEARA PENINSULA
(2–3M)
Earl for a Day, p. 14

Bantry is a pretty market town at the beginning of the Beara Peninsula, overlooking Bantry Bay in West Cork. It is dominated by the Bantry House and Gardens, one of Ireland's great early 18th-century houses. Home to the White family since 1739, the house is huge, with an eclectic collection of priceless European antiques scattered throughout its ornate, plaster-ceilinged rooms and halls. But it's a stroll in the glorious gardens that will give you the most pleasure. They were designed to reflect the best in European design, and as a place for the earl to show off his knowledge of the world's flora. Nine luxurious rooms in the wings are available for overnight stays, with a private dining room and a wood-paneled billiard room for guests' use. The main part of the house is open to the public in the daytime, but in the evening, overnight guests can have the deserted grounds and building to themselves. The peninsula is just as appealing but much less crowded in summer than its more famous neighbors.

CONTACT Bantry House, Bantry, Co. Cork, tel. 027/50047, fax 027/50795. 9 rooms. Restaurant, bar. Double £150–£170, single £85–£95. Closed mid-Nov.–mid-Mar.

DISTANCES 320 km (200 mi) from Dublin, 80 km (50 mi) from Cork City

OPTIONS Sea View House is another, less grand manor overlooking the bay. This three-story Victorian used to be Kathleen O'Sullivan's private home, and she keeps it as if it still were: All the brass shines, the antiques smell of polish, and every guest is treated like an old friend. Try to secure a bedroom with a sea view so you can relax in your bay window seat and contemplate the waves. The wooded grounds are perfect for constitutionals. Ballylickey, near Bantry, Co. Cork, tel. 027/50073, fax 027/51555. 16 rooms. Restaurant, bar, horseback riding. Double £120, single £80.

IN SEARCH OF THE FARMHOUSE CHEESE OF WEST CORK (3M–N)
Eating Your Greens, p. 48

The Southwest is a hot spot for farmhouse and organic foods, and Gubbeen Farm and the nearby harbor town of Schull are at its center. Six generations of Fergusons have lived in the area, and the whole family is dedicated to preserving local foodmaking traditions. The emphasis is on quality versus mass-producibility—a philosophy shared by many of the area's small-scale producers of cheese, bacon, preserves, smoked fish, and so on. You could plan an informal tour of West Cork going from one to another, sampling their hospitality and filling your picnic basket as you go. But don't miss out on dining in small, laid-back Schull, at the beginning of the Mizen Head peninsula. For decades popular with German and French expatriates, the place is an intriguing mix of rural Irish and adventurous cosmopolitan, and much of the local organic produce ends up on the tables of some chic little restaurants. The town can get a bit hectic in July and August but is perfect in the shoulder seasons.

CONTACT Gubbeen House, Schull, Co. Cork, tel./fax 028/28231 (please call before visiting), e-mail: gubbeen@eircom.net, westcorkweb.ie/gubbeen. Tourist Information Office, Grand Parade, Co. Cork, tel. 021/427–3251, fax 021/427–3504. Useful site: www.schull.ie.

DISTANCES Schull is 107 km (67 mi) from Cork City.

OPTIONS Jeffa Gill also produces a classic farmhouse cheese, from cattle grazed on the hills overlooking Dunmanus Bay. Durrus Farmhouse Cheese, Durrus, Bantry, Co. Cork, tel. 027/61100, fax 027/61017. With her husband, Tim, Ireland's famous TV chef Darina Allen runs the **Ballymaloe Cookery School.** Courses range from a day to 12 weeks; accommodation in their country house on an organic farm is included. Shanagarry, Midleton, Co. Cork, tel. 021/464–6785, fax 021/464–6909, www.ballymaloe-cookery-school.ie. Both Shaw and painter Jack Yeats stayed at Schull's **Grove House,** and from your bedroom window you too can enjoy the trawlers bobbing in the harbor. Billy O'Shea, a founding member of the local Slow Food movement, puts on a gourmet spectacular every morning, with perhaps a farmhouse cheese plate, smoked bacon from Gubbeen, Woodcock smoked salmon, fish tartare from just down the road, and Grove's own brown bread. Colla Rd., Schull, Co. Cork, tel. 028/28067, fax 028/28069, www.corkguide.ie/schull/grove/welcome.html. 5 rooms. Double £60–£80, single £40–£50, breakfast included. Closed Nov.–Jan. In the center of town, with snug rooms overlooking the harbor and a restaurant with a patio garden, the family-run **East End** hotel is great value for money. Schull, Co. Cork, tel. 028/28101, fax 028/28012. 17 rooms, 15 with bath. Double £90, single £65. Closed Dec. 23–27.

SOUTHWEST HIGHLIGHTS
The **Ring of Kerry** (2—M) and the **Dingle Peninsula** (1–2L–M) are among the top destinations for visitors to Ireland. As you drive around them, majestic sea views assail you from every side, the land suddenly climbs through treacherous passes and over mountains, and five or six whitewashed houses plus one pub can often constitute an entire village. Favorite stops on the Ring include tiny **Glenbeigh** (2L), with a reconstructed bog-village museum, and the shopping town of **Cahirciveen** (1M). Though a trip to the **Lakes of Killarney** (3L), a stunning tapestry of heather-clad hills and deep-blue lakes dotted with wooded isles, is a must, avoid Killarney itself, a once picturesque town now spoiled by commercialism. Stay instead in busy **Dingle Town** (1L) or the pretty 19th-century market town of **Kenmare** (3M). On Dingle, near the quiet town of Ventry (1L), is the Iron Age **promontory fort of Dunbeg**. Try to visit one of the many islands off the Cork and Kerry coast; the **Blasket** group (1L) is the most interesting, with spectacular scenery and beaches, abundant wildlife, and eerie remains of long-abandoned communities.

THE SOUTHEAST

Stretching from mountainous Wicklow in the north down to flat, warm Wexford and Waterford, and including Kilkenny and Carlow, the "sunny Southeast" is popular with holidaying Irish for its good weather and long sandy beaches. In fact, the virtues of both have been exaggerated: The weather is never reliable in Ireland, and the area's beaches are often overcrowded. The real magic of this region lies in its medieval history. Facing England and the rest of Europe, the Southeast has long been a center for foreign trade and invasion. Wicklow's 6th-century Glendalough, one of a number of Christian monastic sites in the area, ranks next to Clonmacnoise as the country's most important. Three hundred years later the Vikings—attracted by the wealth of such clerical treasures and by the fertile land—founded the towns of Waes-

fjord (Wexford) and Vadrefjord (Waterford). In the 12th century the Normans invaded, choosing the area around Hook Head in Waterford as their beachhead; great stone builders, they left a chain of magnificent castles, walled towns, and ruined churches all across the landscape.

A LIGHTHOUSE STAY ON WICKLOW HEAD (9H)
Closer to Heaven, p. 32

Built in 1781, the lighthouse was originally lit by 20 tallow candles and a large reflector in the eight-sided lantern. The Irish Landmark Trust acquired the long-abandoned property in 1996 and spent two years converting it. It now sleeps six (two double bedrooms and a sofabed). The place has a refreshing, uncluttered feel, with stone walls plastered and painted white and a minimalist approach to furnishings, like cast-iron beds and pine tables painted duck-egg blue. Area maps and sea and star charts allow you to use the telescope to spot the surrounding sights, terrestrial and stellar.

CONTACT Irish Landmark Trust, 25 Eustace St., Temple Bar, Dublin 2, tel. 01/670–4733, fax 01/670–4887, e-mail: landmark@iol.ie, www.irishlandmark.com. Weekly: £500–£800. 3/4 nights Oct.–May: £300/£400.

DISTANCES 2 km (1½ mi) south of Wicklow Town, 53 km (33 mi) south of Dublin

OPTIONS The Garden County of Ireland is full of unique, naturally stunning places to stay. In Rathnew (9H), not far from the Mount Usher Gardens, is **Tinakilly House**, a lovingly restored 1870 Italianate mansion filled with four-poster beds and Jacuzzis with mountain views. The garden provides vegetables for the French-influenced dining room. Rathnew, Co. Wicklow, tel. 0404/69274 or 800/525–4800, fax 0404/67806, www.tinakilly.ie. 12 rooms, 40 suites. Bar, tennis court. Double £192, single £120, breakfast included. **Hunter's Hotel,** one of Ireland's oldest coaching inns, dates from the early 1700s. It sits on the banks of the gentle River Varty, just east of Rathnew. Big-beamed ceilings, period furniture, and flower-print wallpaper give the place a homey, old-fashioned feel. On summer days, tea and cakes are served in the glorious garden, stretching down to the river. Rathnew, Co. Wicklow, tel. 0404/40106, fax 0404/40338. 16 rooms. Restaurant, bar. Double £130, single £85.

A COTTAGE STAY IN THE SOUTHEAST

In Strongbow's Shadow, p. 44

The cottage stay is a specialty in the Southeast. In the Slade cottage, stuffed owls and other birds of prey peer down from every shelf; old buoys and lobster pots hanging on the walls remind you that this was once home to folk who looked to the sea for their livelihoods. Still today you might wake to the noise of the few remaining local boats landing their catch on the harbor wall. They'll sell you fresh crab, lobster, herring, and plaice straight off their decks at a great price. The views are out over lonely, proud Hook Head at the back, and into the communal courtyard (shared with two other cottages) out front—a godsend if you have children. The grass play area is a magnet for friendly local kids, dominated as it is by the ruins of an old Norman castle. On a clear night watch stars gather over the turret of the old fort.

CONTACT Shamrock Cottages, 13 Clifford Terr., Wellington, Somerset TA21 8PQ, England, tel. 011/44–1823–660126, fax 011/44–1823–660125, www.shamrockcottages.co.uk. 3-bedroom cottage (sleeps 4–6). Summer, U.K.£312; off-season, U.K.£156.

DISTANCES 20 km (12½ mi) east of Waterford, 18 km (98 mi) south of Dublin

OPTIONS Cottage stays are available throughout Wexford and Waterford counties. Common factors tend to be traditional old dwellings, easy access to the sea, and interesting historical sites nearby. Shamrock Cottages (see Contact, above) is a major renter of cottages in the area, including **Kiely's,** just outside Ardmore (6L), a village with a number of high-quality properties. Built in the traditional white-washed, thatched-roof fashion common in pre-famine Ireland, Kiely's (2 bedrooms; U.K.£183–U.K.£284) is cozy with low ceilings, turf-burning fireplace, and small, porthole-like windows set into thick walls. Tramore (7K) and Dunmore East (8K) offer more traditional seaside stays—good for the kids, perhaps, but don't expect solitude.

SOUTHEAST HIGHLIGHTS

Two of Wicklow's finest stately homes are **Powerscourt** (9H), with gardens considered among Europe's best and a wonderful waterfall, and **Russborough House** (8H), with impressive vestiges of a once superb private art collection. **Bray** (9G), an old-style seaside resort on the border with Dublin, has a long boardwalk; Bray Head, a hill with sweeping views over the city, is a favorite destination for local walkers. The 137 km (85 mi) **Wicklow Way** is a hiking trail starting near Dublin and crossing the heart of the mountainous county, with cozy B&Bs along the way. **Ardmore** (6L), a delightful village near the Waterford–Cork border, with early medieval roots and 12th-century monastic ruins, boasts one of the 70 remaining round towers in Ireland. The Southeast has a number of major Norman towns, including Carlow (7–8I), Waterford (7K), Wexford (9J), and Kilkenny (7J). All have churches, castles, and graveyards worth seeing, but **Kilkenny Castle,** dating from 1391, is perhaps the finest in Ireland. The **Ring** (7K) is an isolated Irish-speaking region on Dungarvan Bay; the nearby bogs and mountains are perfect for hiking, and the town of **Dungarvan** (7K) is a popular resort and fishing spot.

New York–based photographer Simon Russell jumped into the travel-photography seat 10 years ago and has kept the pedal to the metal ever since. This is his second Escape book for Fodor's, and if his wife allows, it won't be his last escape to some exotic locale. He has been published in *National Geographic Traveler, Trips, Blue, The New York Daily News, Condé Nast Traveler,* and other publications worldwide. His first adventure in Ireland, in 1986, was to renovate a castle and mansion for a friend, although drinking Guinness at the local pub and snapping photographs took precedence. This latest journey through the heart of the Emerald Isle opened his eyes to the passion the Irish people have for life and the tales spun around the pub roundtable.

Anto Howard was born on the Northside of Dublin, where people have a terrible habit of abbreviating perfectly good names and sticking an *o* on the end of them. He was educated in the heart of the city at Trinity College Dublin. On graduation he headed off to New York, determined to seek out everything except his fortune. He became a travel writer and visited 44 states, plus most of Central America and Canada. But home was always calling, and in early 2000 he returned to Ireland. Lucky for him that was just when the idea for the Escape book came up, and he jumped on board. Visiting almost every county in Ireland while researching the book gave him a great opportunity to reacquaint himself with the land he had left behind.